× ×

YEAR GONE HAZY

Send-offs to 2020

Edited by: Josue Caceres
Cover by: Amaurys Grullon

Published in 2020 by
BX Writers
Bronx Native
127 Lincoln Ave
Bronx, NY 10454
info@bronxnative.com
josue@bronxnative.com

Please email josue@bronxnative.com for bulk
purchases or further information.

Edited by: Josue Caceres
Cover by: Amaurys Grullon

Bronx Brewery
856 E 136th St
Bronx, NY 10454
thebronxbrewery.com

Other books published by BX Writers:
BX Writers Anthology Vol. 1

Backcover Photo:
Remy Goza
@remygoza

CONTENTS

Summary 1

Foreword by: The Bronx Brewery/
Kevin Scheitrum 2

Constance Smith 8

Miqueas Molano 9

Raidy.. 10

Clare 11

James S. Alvarez 12

Diego C 13

Courtneay Fitts 14

Damil Canales 16

Sean Twist 17

Anabel Encarnación 18

Adrian Rodriguez 19

Sarah Caro 20

Johansel Estrella 21

Alexis Garcia 22

Travis 23

Josué Caceres 24

Natalia 25

Mary Ana McKay 26

Imani Jones 27

AJ Keirans 28

Harry Ott 29

David Michaelson 30

Eddin 31

Sabrina Merchant 32

David Figueroa 33

Bernard Kaplan 34

Ben Cathers 35

Dan 36

Skyler Reid 37

Stefano 38

Guadalupe Lopez 39

Ryan Olsen 40

Synthia 41

George Gardner 42

Yaslin Espinal 43

Idalia Soto 44

Brandon Espinosa 45

Ian Boswell 46

Laplace Stern 47

Zinzi 48

Steven Poser 49

Fernando Liz 50

Victor 51

Josh Rivera 52

Kyle Naranjo 53

Bella Foxx 54

Joel C 55

Jonathan Marin 56

Olufemi Watson 57

Danelvi 58

Majora 59

Claudia Brown 60

Destiny 61

CentriQ 62

Magi Camaj 63

Opal Abreu 64

Richard Scholz 65

Rosanna Razack 66

Erika Torres 68

Patrick Benedict 69

Bruce BLUE Rivera 70

Blue Rivera 71

Anny Mariano 72

Marta 73

T'Asia J. Holmes 74

Erica Usurin 75

Em 76

Luisa Lo 77

Stephanie Ortiz 78

Jennifer Arocha 79

Ashley 80

Taye Thomas 81

Yaddy Valerio 82

Chelsey Macklin 83

Ameresoul 84

George Brown 87

Jenny 88

Taiitan 89

Dena 90

Sonyi Lopez 91

Mara 92

Janeth Perla 93

Tim Shields 94

Yohancey Kingston 95

Erica 96

Erika 97

V. I. Reyes 98

Joan Vargas 99

Javette McCoy 101

Selina Feng 102

Will 103

Marlin Santana 104

Alexandra Nazario 107

Rosy Garcia 108

Jamie Baugh 109

Robert Perry 110

Savannah Miles 111

Jorge 112

Sadeka Harris 113

Derek Coy 114

Damian Brown 115

Lizzette Nuñez 116

Billy Manton 117

Amy Mendez 118

Damaris Lopez 119

Jordan Jones 120

KD 121

John MacCarthy 122

Derrick Z. Jackson 123

Kenyon Taylor 124

Greg Miranda 125

Gabby 126

Marie 127

Keva G 128

Laurie Jane 129

Karyn 130

Gabriel Rosangel 131

Marysol 132

John Zufall 133

Mark Brown 134

Steven Waxman 135

Yvonne 136

Anonymous Bronx Girl 137

Jennifer Pinilla 138

Aric Yackly 139

ATABEY 140

Miosotty Hiciano 141

Miguelina 144

Chi Chen 146

Leanne Stella 147

Kirstie Saunders 148

King Neptune 149

J Roddy 150

Zelina Martinez 151

Bronx Antics 152

Julissa Contreras 153

Daniel Lanzilotta 155

Jen 156

Joe Rienti 157

Yasmilka Clase 158

Elias Ortiz 160

Faith Sone 161

Bianca Guzman 162

Madeline Ramos 163

Josue Mendez 164

Ammara 165

Melissa Caraballo 166

Natasha Garcia 167

Jasmine 168

Diego Leon 169

theViine 170

Laraine 172

Jessica Diaz 173

Carlos Matias 174

Jake Alrich 176

Steven Almeida 177

Bryan Orbe 178

DèLise Temple 179

Ruddy Mejia 180

Julio Jordan 181

Esther Rosa 183

Uni-G 184

Kimberly 185

Maurice Hurd 186

Bishop 187

Sonia 188

Kevin Scheitrum 189

Amaurys Grullon 190

Haneiro Perez 191

Message from the team 193

Bio/Resources 196

SUMMARY

The Bronx Brewery, BX Writers and Bronx Native are coming together to wave goodbye to 2020 with a limited-edition beer and a book, featuring sendoffs to 2020 from across New York, the country and around the world.

Called 'Year Gone Hazy', the double dry-hopped, double IPA will publish hundreds of Love Letters to 2020 across each 16oz 4-pack. A spinoff of the brewery's popular World Gone Hazy IPA.

The responses went on to also be printed on sweaters and published in a year-end book by BX Writers and Bronx Native, who most recently launched the BX Writers Anthology; a bound, hardcover showcase of Bronx-based writers and poets.

FOREWORD

As the years pile up, eventually you start to suspect that nothing is ever just one thing. Even the worst year ever. Especially the worst year ever.

We're living in this age of forced simplicity. Not only because of social media but, yeah, mainly because of social media. Rage to drive revenue. The whole human experience, reduced to extremes. Basically, it's like being in high school again.

It all makes it easy to forget what time teaches us: that every decision we make, every experience we live, every person we meet - they all contain multitudes, like Walt Whitman said, "Layers unfolding into layers." Like Shrek said, "Nothing's as simple as it seems."

So while 2020 can be summed up in a word -- for the rest of our lives, tens of millions of us will think of 2020 when we hear 'lockdown' or 'pandemic' or 'Cuomo' or 'Fauci' or 'worst f*cking year ever' (it's one word if you say it fast) Shorthand doesn't do justice to this year.

Which is why we were so proud to work on this project with our friends at Bronx Native & BX Writers. Because this year, too, contained multitudes. And we didn't want these lived experiences - these long days and these vanishing months, this clarity and confusion, these stories we've told ourselves to get through to disappear. To be reduced to a single word or a single feeling by time.

Because too much happened to let that happen. And while this year was awful (and it really was awful), it was so much more than that. So many stood up and made sacrifices for this city, their loved ones and their neighbors. So many stood up and marched against injustice, working tirelessly to push for a better world. So many people had their entire worlds upended, only to rise up again and again.

We all made those essential, critical small decisions every day to just keep moving forward. We lived through a year that united us in these big ways. Quarantine. Existential Dread. Zoom...****ing Zoom. But (and I think you felt this too), it was the small, super-specific things that really made you feel closer to strangers. Stuff like the knowing nod behind a mask or the hurry to put one on when you get within 10 feet of somebody on an NYC street. Or not wearing pants for months.

At the brewery, like our GM Brandon always says, "We're in this incredible position to be able to meet people at their highest points and often, their lowest. Celebrating on a great day- commiserating on a bad one. And we feel unbelievably fortunate to be able to play a role, however small, in people's lives." To quote our president Damian, "That's why we get up every day." But we also see it as a responsibility.

We know that in order to mean something, you have to listen, constantly. To be a platform, you have to be a participant. That's why we put our community at the center of everything we do, and we're beyond honored to have your words on our beer and inside this book. To give a glimpse into the year that was from 200 different voices.

There are all sorts of ways to describe this year from one grand perspective. But they all gloss over those small moments and tiny connections we've shared. The ones that kept us connected, the ones that inspired us and the ones that reminded us how much we need each other.

This is a book about the small stuff.

The Bronx Brewery/ Kevin Scheitrum

What do you want to say to 2020?

Talk about tough love.
Survival. Fear. The "grind." Gotta make it,
gotta stay up. Needing and not having.
Having less than enough and making it
work. It has to. Making us work.
We "have" to.
You gave us an opportunity to slow down.
To reflect, to release, to reimagine.
A chance to journey back inside long enough
to meet ourselves again, though it still feels
strange. You allowed us to see that we are
small beings with magnificent reach.

A year of insurmountable pain and suffering
and equally as much revolutionary joy.
Have we ever loved THIS hard? I have felt
and now I choose to release the pain, the
hurt, the shame. I'm grateful for the beauty
and good times and big lessons that can't be
undone. You are my shadow and I bravely
face you, so that there's more light in the
world after we're through.

Constance Smith
IG/Twitter- @cruelladabillz

Thank you for filtering out the fake friends, didn't need to use a pandemic to do it though.

You survived a whole pandemic yet you stressed about finals?

Miqueas Molano
IG- @Mangata96

2020 - 0 ; The People - 1

No matter how many lives you took,
disasters you caused, lies and social
destruction were thrown our way.
The sheer will of the human spirit
(we the people), especially us New Yorkers,
was never and will never be defeated.
We are NY tough.

Raidy
IG- @Raidy.Moon
Twitter- @Raidy_moon

I fell in love when the pandemic
displaced me;
shoutout @Bumble

One of Covid's effects was being displaced
from my college housing. I did NOT want to
move home after graduation but that's just
how it went. Out of sheer boredom, I started
swiping on the dating apps. And then I met
someone. We 'virtually' dated until it was
safer to meet up. We streamed The Front
Bottoms on Twitch. We took a virtual tour of
the Georgia Aquarium. We got creative and
fell in love. I couldn't imagine my world
without him now. He's my silver lining.

Clare
IG- @AmericanBlondeAle
Twitter- @ABAtweetin

11

Fuhgeddaboutdit

I drink beer, so what.

James S. Alvarez

Thank you for being flavorful.
You gave us a taste of everything this year.

We're thankful for your flavor. You gave us a
taste of it all. Your entrée introduced us to
the bitter of unrest, the sour of corruption,
and the spice of a revolution. These juices all
dance on our tongues, an aftertaste we can't
seem to rinse. But should we? Never
forgotten is the first swig, the first puff, nor
the first lips. These are the tastes that define
us. Welcome to the collection, 2020.

Diego C.
IG- @decleridan

WHAT THE FU** HAPPENED?!

Dear Year 2020,

I'm sure you are already expecting or even anticipating this question, but WHAT THE FUCK HAPPENED?!

You were supposed to be the YEAR! You were supposed to stand out amongst all the others. You were supposed to transform us. You were supposed to show us the true meaning of the quote "life is short." You were supposed to remove the veil that has been cast over our eyes for some time now. You were supposed to give us a break. You were supposed to give us some time to eat, think and pray. You were supposed to let me work on my craft and enjoy doing all the things that I am actually passionate about. You were supposed to remind us of the importance of family. You were supposed to show us who our REAL friends are. You were supposed to remind us that racism still exists. You were supposed to teach us how to evolve physically, mentally and financially. You were supposed to teach us to appreciate even the smallest things in life. You were supposed to show us just how evil and corrupt our world leaders are. You were supposed to spread fear. You were supposed to give us strength and courage. You were supposed to give us a voice. You were supposed to ignite some fire up under all of our asses and force us to stand up and TAKE ACTION!

Wait. What am I saying? You did all of those things and more.
THANK YOU 2020

Sincerely,
Someone Who Chooses LOVE over LOATHING.

Courtneay Fitts
IG- @centriq

Thanks for the memories (good and bad) and thanks for all the things you taught me about myself and others. You made your point. We'll be better. We promise.

Damil Canales
IG/Twitter- @Sixsauce

As terrible a year as 2020 was for many reasons, I am lucky enough to say I've found a woman I love, started my Master's degree, learned to appreciate the little things in life, and turned all the negatives 2020 brought me into positives

Sean Twist
IG/Twitter- @seantwiiist

17

2020 is love disguised as loss.

Anabel Encarnación
IG- @anabelencarnaci0n

No matter the situation never let your
emotions over power your intelligence.
2020 has been the year about mental battles.
For those who lost love ones stay strong.
For those who survive. Be happy. Be positive
and always smile.

Adrian Rodriguez
IG- @Beerhoppybros

Broken champagne bottles & frozen clocks,
but we see confettied hope and our
reflections in the shards.

Sarah Caro
IG- @thensarahwrites

20

Overwhelming but I found my true self

In 2020 we found our crafts,
we found our life goals,
we had a chance to work on what we love,
but we lost many of our people!!

Johansel Estrella
IG- @writerforthevoiceless

I Salute You, 2020!

Alexis Garcia
IG- @lexiegee
Twitter- @lexiegee333

Online shipped

Ever since the Covid hit,
we all had to hunker down,
except for essential workers,
we had to do our part.
From the medical fields, to the beer
industries

Travis
IG- @845_beerguy

2020 I'm back out of my coma!

Josué Caceres
IG- @josue_caceres

Still had a good time,
glad you weren't here for a long time.

Sometimes you lose because you need to be
humbled and pushed in another direction.
Either you win or learn.
We needed this lesson.
Thank you.

Natalia
IG- @incogsmashdoe
Twitter- @smashianna

You can't have it all

2020, you took a lot, but you can't have it all.
You took my uncle, you took my dreams,
you took my hope, you took my happiness.
You took so much from so many and didn't
even bat an eye. You wasted our goddamn
time pretending things might get better, only
to drain us more. You get no sympathy when
we leave you in the dust, so here, have your
time, because you won't get anything else
from us.
You tried to take so much,
but you can't have it all.

Mary Ana McKay
IG/Twitter- @Sistersharpie

New World Order

The masks on our faces went on as the inner
masks came off.
Uncovering of bottle caps and cork screws
ignited the truth serum to flow from the lips
of the one's in charge.

Imani Jones
IG- @thehippymom

Just when you think it can't get any worse,
you realize it's only Tuesday.

AJ Keirans
IG/Twitter- @16ozCanvas

If life is up then you are down.

Harry Ott
IG/Twitter- @meemsone

Goodbye to a year of bad vision

David Michaelson

Only Godzilla at the hub could've made this worse.

Eddin
IG/Twitter- @ThankYouEddin

Year gone hazy,
but NYC isn't dead, it's TOUGH.

Sabrina Merchant
IG/Twitter- @pocketsizesabs

2020, get the F**K OUTTA HERE!!!

David Figueroa

Please let the horror end.
I want to go back to the Bronx and my beer!

I was born in the Bronx in 1944.
It will always be home. When my wife and I
visited the Bronx Brewery we fell in love
with the place. And with the beer of course.
We have been stuck in NJ because of our risk
of Covid. I want/need to get back to God's
borough and beer. We love you folks.

Bernard Kaplan

Thank you 2020 for affirming I will always love NY

Even during one of the toughest years ever, quarantine, community and resilience were all on display in NYC. It made me realize, even more than ever, that this is truly my home and where I always will want to be. The response, the recovery and the community in NYC is truly second to none.

I remember during the first part of quarantine, craving any sense of normalcy, and walking 3 miles from the Upper East Side to the Bronx Brewery. Being able to grab beers and see a business operating, gave me hope we can get through this.

Ben Cathers
IG/Twitter- @bencathers

2020, you are temporary
Bronx Brewery is forever and the
Wu-Tang Clan!

Dan
IG- @jibaroviajero
Twitter- @jibaroviajero13

Well, that sucked.

Skyler Reid
IG/Twitter- @Skyreid

Dear 2020, Thank you for going away.

Stefano
IG- @justanotherbarros

You tested us to our limit and brought us to our knees yet here we stand. Through the haze you made us see what's really important. For that I thank you but I'm so glad to see you go.
#HastaNunca2020 #NYStrong

Guadalupe Lopez

Sometimes things won't be ok

Ryan Olsen
IG/Twitter- @olyrc

LIFE LINE- Living Is For Ever,
Learning Is Never Ending

Synthia
IG- @miss_syn

So long 2020, you were empty and petty,
I'll use my machete to make you confetti.
Then I'll be ready & steady for a Bronx Ale
with the cognoscenti.

George Gardner

the chaos ignited a light to awake what was
dormant in us

You brought a moment of stillness
where I couldn't avoid myself anymore
all the distractions that danced around
in the hallways of my thoughts
no longer had a home
you made me say goodbye
to what i once knew
so that i can make room
for the things that spoke my truth
for the things i thought i did not deserve
for the person i didn't think i can become

Although, you came in darkness,
you later showed a light i haven't quite seen
before.
a light needed, to awake what was dormant
in me. thank you.

Yaslin Espinal
IG- @Yassslin

You thought you could beat me but I don't
give up

This year has been full of challenges but that
has forced me to grow and adapt in ways that
I never thought possible. I know I am
stronger than ever because I faced each
challenge and overcame them. I will let go of
the pain you caused and look toward the
opportunities you gave me.

Idalia Soto
IG/Twitter- @Ladollie

Thank you for the memories!
I am stronger because of it.

Brandon Espinosa
IG- @brandonjespi

Slainté 2020, You Rat Bastard

Ian Boswell
IG/Twitter- @ianboswell93

2020に対して、日本語でsayonaraとは言わなく「kutabare」と言う。非常に美しいことなのだ。

Laplace Stern
Twitter- @laplaceinplace

Creative$ Never Die

No te olvides de lavarte las manos
y la lengua hoy

Zinzi
IG- @zinzabell @auxcordzbx
Twitter- @zinzabell

2020 Time Capsules - Not a thing.

There once was a year 2020,
With Covid, Politics and hate aplenty,
So happy it's gone,
For a New Years Day dawn,
I know 21 will treat us more gently!

Steven Poser
Twitter- @metsfan4ever_41

2020 SMD From The BACK

Fernando Liz
IG- @Pronando

This time it's you, 2020.
Just remember to leave the keys when you leave.
And don't forget to take your friend with you!

Victor
IG- @TheHernandez5

You deadass tried your hardest to break me,
too bad I'm NY tough

Josh Rivera
IG/Twitter- @JoshJustDidIt

Good Riddance

Kyle Naranjo
IG/Twitter- @kyle_naranjo

Good-bye 2020,
you were a very bad year for a lot of good
people, and some bad people,
but I don't really care about them because
they were very bad.
Which is a very mean thing for me to say I
admit.
But yeah, go away, don't come back.

Bella Foxx
IG/Twitter- @nycphotoues

Need the biggest Resolution with a side of
No Resolution.

I thought 2020 was the worst year of my life.
It's been quite the paradox. Sometimes what
we deem as being lost was supposed to be
part of the journey all along. It's all a draft
until you die. (see what I did there?)
Cheers to The Bronx and all of my friends +
family.

Joel C.
IG/Twitter- @ItsJfuse

For 365 days some suffered, some prospered,
while others felt hopeless.
But it was beer that kept us together.

Jonathan Marin
IG/Twitter- @thebronxpulse

Hindsight is 2020

This year has taught me a lot (and I hope it did the same for others) and tested me in ways I didn't think possible.
We have to move forward with what we learned, for a better future. Here's to a bright & prosperous 2021.

Also I just want this year in the distance of my rear view.

Olufemi Watson
IG- @fem.de.la.creme
Twitter- @SpicedCelestial

You were a bitch, but I loved you!

Danelvi
IG- @Itsdanelvi

Talent Retention

You don't have to move out of your neighborhood to live in a better one

Majora
IG- @Boogiedowngrind
Twitter- @Majoracarter

Challenged but Not Defeated!

Cheers to beer and not another virus year!

Claudia Brown

Thanks for teaching me resilience...
but bye girl.

Destiny

2020 was like the last season of
Game of Thrones...
We Need A Reshoot!

CentriQ a.k.a. Courtneay Fitts
IG- @centriq

Letters to 2020,
Thank you.
The hardships you possessed,
was nothing we couldn't get through.

Internal war.
External war.

Yeah it hurt,
but we got stronger within,
and now we have a deeper appreciation
and a more beautiful world view.
NYC taught us
that in the hard times,
although broken,
we were each other's glue.

Fighting for health,
Fighting for equality,
You taught us a lot--
one main thing is that
when we come together,
ANYTHING
we can get through.

Love,
MC

Magi Camaj
IG- @magicamaj
Twitter- @shewrotemagic

Attached.

Opal Abreu
IG- @_opalsur
Twitter- @_Suriell

Beer in one hand, confidence in the other

I remember when you walked into Bierkraft
over 10 years ago and later told me you were
inspired to start the brewery from the talk
we had.

Richard Scholz
IG- @richard.l.scholz

Dear 2020,

You tried to f**k me, so I just changed positions. Sounds like a weird way to put it, right? You threw curveballs at me that I wasn't ready for. Those curveballs came in the form of the pain and hurt that I hid from myself through day to day distractions. Every day of quarantine, I woke up feeling like I was asphyxiating on the memories of hurt; a broken heart, my childhood and sexual trauma. I had lost myself. The woman in the mirror was unrecognizable to me. And I had to find Rose again. 2020, I hated you because you put me in a position where I had no choice but to confront the aches in my heart. And it was hard. Boy, was it hard. Hard enough to want to wish myself out of this Universe. But one day, in the blur of days that was quarantine, I woke up and I decided to get help. Help that I was apprehensive about getting. Being an Indo Caribbean woman, I always had the narrative that therapy was for "crazy" people. But it's not true, it never was. I wasn't crazy. I was just hurt. And hurt people hurt other people, including themselves. So before I had the chance to cause anymore hurt, I decided to transmute this pain. Pain that I had kept in the depths of my heart for so long. I needed to become Rose again. I used this time to love myself again. In a way that I never did before, as it was discomforting to actually love myself without feeling guilty. Months later, I think about that woman I was in January 2020, and I saw someone so broken. But I used this unfortunate time to fill the cracks in her heart with light. And as I write this, the day before my 28th birthday (Nov. 3), I recognized that while 2020 did ruin a lot of my plans, COVID took many lives and tested the mental, physical and economic well-being of those left behind. I was brought back to myself. I was able to love who I was completely. And for that, I will always be grateful.

Rosanna Razack
IG- @scorpio.dreamin

It was clear as day, no clouds.
Darkness overcame.
I stood tall. Grounded.
Rain fell & I asked myself how much can I
take?
My roots continued to serve as an anchor.
I blossomed new leaves throughout the
uncertainty.
Partial clouds gave a sense of hope.
A ray of sunshine then beamed down and
touched my hard exterior.
I stand tall. Grounded.
I couldn't be more thankful to have survived.

Erika Torres
IG- @ev.tee
Twitter- @evtee_

Priorities shifted this year.
I value family, friendship, honesty, and
decency.
I want my son to grow up in a world of
peace, equality, and justice.

Patrick Benedict
IG- @benedictbeerblog
Twitter- @PatrickBenedict

No matter the obstacles or darkest days
We're united as a community.
Together We Can!

Bruce BLUE Rivera
IG/Twitter- @MissionHHNyc

The cavalry ain't coming!!!!
It's time for us to save our communities
ourselves.

Blue Rivera
IG/Twitter- @Blueyorkcity

In 2020, I wanted to crush a can of beer with
my hands more than once.
To prevent a mess, I drank out of chilled
glass instead.
Now, I sip in joy knowing I still don't know
what day it is. Cheers!

Anny Mariano
IG- @name.isanny

Thank you for helping me find love for the first time in a person I wouldn't have met otherwise. Also for pushing me to love myself first no matter what.

Marta
IG- @marta_ellen

2020 made you BLUE?
Cure that shit with some BRONX BREW,
4get what 2020 did 2 U!

T'Asia J. Holmes
IG- @Okayitztay
Twitter- @okayitztay1527

TY 2020 for finally letting me live my dream introvert life.

Proud of my fellow Bronxites for wearing masks this whole time and being essential for helping the city stay open.

Erica Usurin
IG/Twitter- @ethevoyeur

During this crazy year NYC showed me every day why I love its strength, resilience and people. As a native New Yorker I've never felt more connected to every single person in this city than I did when we all had to band together and show sympathy, empathy and courtesy to the thousands that were hurting or dying because of COVID. No matter where I go in the world, New York City and its impenetrable force will always be a part of me.

Em
IG- @thehungrydominican
Twitter- @hungrydominican

Dear 2020, in the words of Selena,
"No me queda mas."

While I believe there is still good in the
world, 2020 you have tested us in many ways
and I am happy to leave you behind. I will
however take the lessons of holding my
family and friends close, not taking everyday
things for granted, and appreciating my
physical and mental wellness.
Pero ya... No te quiero ver mas.

Luisa Lo
IG- @luisalora

THANK GOODNESS IT'S OVER!!
WE SOMEHOW MADE IT!
2021 PLS BE GOOD TO US

Stephanie Ortiz
IG/Twitter- @Infamous_stefii

The Year of Courage

We cheered for you to have more life, health
and love with family.
A pandemic disease spreading in the midst
of broken fans losing a legend from the
Lakers.
We were forced to stay at home, while
distancing was strongly encouraged,
We grew closer to our families,
To ourselves,
To our mental health.
We lost some along the way to a virus and
police inequality,
But our voices have been stronger than ever.
Our strength will drive us through this year.
Our voices will continue to be heard through
our voting and peaceful protests.
Our courage will kindly walk you out of our
lives in December.
Even though we weren't prepared for your
events,
We remain strong in knowing whatever else
you throw at us,
We will fight through it, together.

Jennifer Arocha
IG- @xo_jennnn

GOODBYE

While everything about you sucked,
I learned so much about my community,
importance of self-care and gained a furry
addition to my family.
So goodbye to you and hello to our new
lives!

Ashley
IG- @ashleylatwell

Let's not do this again…

Taye Thomas
IG- @temp_taye_tion

Dear 2020, Thank You for the experience.
Now bye bitch!

Yaddy Valerio
IG/Twitter- @Yaddyv_____

Stripped of everything we've ever seen to be true,
we cheers to 2020 as our lens of vision, the mirror, and the light for our eyes to finally open to see that we, as humans, are connected to everything.

Chelsey Macklin
IG- @chelseyville
Twitter- @chelss_smiles

My papa was a hard working man! Worked
until the day he died just to provide, I will
never complain again. 2020 you broke me,
but molded an artist that believes in his
process! Don't sleep on me!

Dear 2020
Can we talk.
Can we converse on how you helped me
write this verse

Rewind to the 1st.
I mean new year new me,
Yeah what a day
where my expectations were of high hopes
No false hope reality
Molding the perfect year.
Making resolutions with no fear.
Promising that this year would be my year.

I've conquered this year as opportunity.
Why did you fool me.
Replacing my heart with broken images
Of things I wasn't ready to see
Replacing the words I made it
with why can't I make it

why does this happen to me

As if I didn't pray hard enough for you not to
throw me another curve ball,
opening day will never be the same.
My father loved the New York Yankees, why
did you choose that day. March 2 to make
him gasp his last piece of air with no one
there!

If I wrote a letter to the New York Yankees
Will they send me there blessings and a
prayer
Just a side thought

2020 you did make me see clearer
I'll give you that.
You showed me that even family can wear
the devils name.
You showed me that trust can go a long way.
You showed me that friendships can be the
biggest mask to hide the true colors away.

In the blink of an eye life will never be same
In the blink of an eye your world can collide

with the alternate reality you're still the
same.
Focus on the last line this rant changes the
game
I love my life either way

Sincerely
-AMERESOUL-

Ameresoul
IG- @Ameresoul

We beerly made it, hoppy new year!

George Brown

Thanks 2020 for not being GOAT and
drowning our hope in tears and beers!

Jenny
IG- @Jenny.jenjenn

Dear 2020 you've taken family, you've taken friends, you've taken ambition, and you've taken time. Too much. But in a way, I'm glad you did. You've shown me importance. The importance of the simple hello's, the passing smiles, the crowded subways, the growing leaves and the falling ones, the little things. Thank you for stopping me in my tracks. Thank you for showing me how bad, bad can get, so that I know how great, great will be.

Living through love, always - Taiitan

Taiitan
IG/Twitter- @Taiitan

this year deadass almost took me out not
quite bitch @ 2020

Dena
IG/Twitter- @denaax3

Cheers,

To those we've mourned.
To those we've lost.
To those we've welcomed.
To those we celebrate.
To those who live within us.
To those we'll never forget.

Dear 2020, nice try trying to tear the Bronx
apart, you only brought us closer together.

Sonyi Lopez
IG- @sovereigngee

NYC for the win.

and scene.

Mara

IG- @mkmig

We're stronger than you!

Janeth Perla
IG- @gloomyperla

At least there's been free beer

Tim Shields
IG/Twitter- @tishield

Thank you for the 2020 vision.
Now time for blurred lines.

Yohancey Kingston
IG/Twitter- @yo_im_hancey

Dear 2020, KiCk RoCkS!

Dear 2020, You broke our hearts

Erica
IG- @Eariasvidal

Go home 2020. You're drunk!

Erika
IG- @Nyc_brunchbabe

Enjoyed the moments of self reflection and self care.

2020 shook the entire world. It made us all pause from a life that many viewed as normal; and watched the demise of our neighbors, friends and loved ones. It showed us how people can be compassionate to each other and help thy neighbor. It raised more awareness that humanity still has a lot of filtering to do with injustice and hate. 2020 has made us prepared for changes some good, some bad. As we evolve from this hazy year let's all toast to change, lost ones, good memories, resilience, better tomorrows and BXB beer. Cheers to the world!
- Mr. Harsh Reality

V. I. Reyes
IG- @Mr_Harsh_Reality

Dear 2020,

I don't regret to inform you that our tumultuous relationship is coming to an end. You have abusively taken my plans and straight trashed them. All the while making me believe this is all my fault. You remind me that I should've appreciated everything before you ball dropped your way into my life. Gaslighting me into thinking that perhaps you are not accountable. I am the one to blame for my depressive state. I lack positivity, perhaps I should smile under the mask you have forced over my mouth. I bet you have masked me not to protect me, but to protect yourself. You fear I'd tell everyone about how you diminished my dreams only to revamp them into creative outlets. The same outlets that make me question, AM I EVEN GOOD ENOUGH?

BEING WITH YOU IS A TOTAL FUCKING ROLLERCOASTER.

You and I are up and down. We fight to only kiss and make up through quarantine nights with candle light dinners serving sautéed poetic lingo. Together with some 'shut the fuck up' wine so that it's the only whining relative to my big mouth. My deserted complaints of how badly you have treated me are rectified as you apologize via the creative content you allow me to generate. Someday you will take credit for that too. Like you've taken credit for my new found gratitude, you've taught me to appreciate all I've had prior to you.

But I got some news for you:

YOU AIN'T SHIT AND I'M LEAVING YOU FOR 2021.

GO TO HELL

Joan Vargas
IG- @Jav_Writes_

Out with the old, in with the new.
2020 guess what, Fuck You.

2020 kicked our ass so out with the old and
in with the new. I don't want to see no more
violence cause it's taking our people and the
virus is killing us too. All I want is that good
thing back, so take me there when life was
good just like this good old beer.

Javette McCoy
IG- @Jaymcc40

2020 - I know we just met but I kinda appreciate you? You're beautifully chaotic. (Still hate you though) xoxo - S.

Selina Feng
IG- @prettylittlefeng

You've broken me. You've left me broke.
You stole happiness and nearly killed us all.
The good never outweighed the bad.
Still we stand. You cannot kill me, mi gente
or our pride. You've done way too much
2020. Change is inevitable. Just wait on it.

Will
IG/Twitter- @willcblogs

20/20 Visions

Fear almost had me
Triggers almost blocked me
Anxiety almost won

I am used to being in the ring with my
thoughts
But this year my mind strategized
Tracking my patterns for months
And when given the opportunity
This bitch gave it all she got
There were no boundaries
No skeletons left unturned
What I thought would be my victory lap
Was my biggest test of perseverance

On pause with no choice but to face things
I threw my hands up
But she already had me
Uppercut
Kobe's death
Left jab
Police brutality
Right jab
COVID-19

Knee in the stomach
Fuck Donald Trump
Blindsided me
Systemic racism is still very much alive in
this country
Pulled my hair
Ending outgrown relationships and habits
Broke my fucking heart
My grandfather's death

Still I stand
With a bloody nose and a black eye
Choosing to take control over what I can
I need you to choose
Choose to leave a legacy
Make glitter out of ashes
You are not your negative thoughts
Be less fear and more hungry to discover
yourself
Be prideful
You have seen things others haven't
2020 gave 20/20 vision
Don't opt into distractions
Comfort
Self-sabotaging your full potential

Choose to be unconditional love in a world
that so desperately needs it
Choose to be you

Marlin Santana (GoodJuju)
IG- @__goodjuju

Thank you for the hellos and the goodbyes,
for the night hugs and the sweet lies 2020

Alexandra Nazario
IG- @Alex.anaz_

Thank you for making me believe and showing me that long distance love is doable and can be very special.
More importantly thank you for giving me the time and forcing the self reflection to love myself more.

I've lived in sweats (ala dem college days) but year 2020 was the year i didn't wear pants from March to November.
Thank you for letting me be creative with my daily outfits which consisted of dresses, skirts and shorts only!

Rose Garcia
IG- @ella.es.rose

Now let me make myself clear
2020 has been THAT year
When you were lonely
Or just wanted a beer
you sent a drunk text
then hooked up with your ex
Me oh my
2020 has been THAT year

Jamie Baugh
IG- @Jamieintheusa
Twitter- @Bciloveyous

Success means nothing, without struggle

Robert Perry
IG- @Robert119
Twitter- @Moretheperrier

My brother Niegel Joshua Aldea (NJA)
passed away in June 2020. He was the most
Bronx man I ever knew.. from the henny to
the timbs. This quote was written by him and
is what resonates with me the most about
2020. We have been through so much
together collectively and individually
through this apocalyptic year but it is in
these difficult times that I am reminded of
the words my brother once spoke "it doesn't
matter what you've been through cus you
can get through, just keep that on the
mental".

Savannah Miles
IG- @Ohhmysav
Twitter- @Sav20Savage

Sus

Jorge
IG- @Prodigal_class

In 2020, we learned to stand together,
even while 6 feet apart.

Sadeka Harris
IG- @Traveldeelite
Twitter- @Partydeelite

2020 proved that the Bronx is still burning...with the same passion to create something beautiful in times of great adversity.

Derek Coy
IG- @ClassicD
Twitter- @ClassicDCoy

2020 hammed home the fact that,
at the end of the day, we all need each other.
Thank you for the lessons of perseverance,
humility and togetherness.

Damian Brown
IG- @leroyandpickle

You helped me realize how important it was
to find my strength, for myself,
for my family,
you can't knock me down!

Lizzette Nuñez
IG- @laqueenbeeme
Twitter- @toughromanchica

In April, when ambulances to Kings County Hospital passed by our apartment nonstop, you were there with me.
I want to thank my wife, without whom I don't know how I would've gotten through those rough months of being an essential worker in the height of NYCs cases.

Billy Manton
IG- @beerboibilly
Twitter- @NarcRuffalo

Good Riddance!!!

Amy Mendez

Thanks, we got through this together.
Bronx strong

Damaris Lopez

2020, you are like a toxic mate,
even though you have been the worst,
you've taught me so much about myself
indirectly in hindsight…

2020 has been a living, breathing
rollercoaster but it has made me stronger
wiser and more compassionate to others,
Shoutout to the Bronx Brew!!!!
This is Dope!!!!

Jordan Jones
IG- @Cooljayjonze

Toodaloo MutherFu*ker

It is what it is (that's easier said for some
than others),
but 2020 came and now it's time for that shit
to pack its fucking bags and toodaloo.

KD
IG/Twitter- @KDwiththebeard

121

2020 is hindsight

John MacCarthy

Avast to Virus, Au Revoir to Racism,
Salud to Democracy

Derrick Z. Jackson
Twitter- @DerrickZJackson

This year has been trying.
Many felt pain, many were left crying.
Many souls vanished and still more people
are dying… Sorrow, hate and death took
over. I can't wait for this f*cking year to be
over. We're hoping for better days, bring on
2021.
2020 brought storms and now we look
forward to the sun.
Brighter days are coming!

Kenyon Taylor
IG- @malcolmflex2011

If you can survive 2020,
you can thrive anywhere.

Dear 2020,
You get no bendicion from me.
You do have my vete pa carajo though.
Don't forget to take Racism and COVID
with you.

Not yours truly,
A BXrican

Greg Miranda
IG- @gregdizciple22
Twitter- @DZG22

Bye 2020, you will not be missed.

Gabby
IG- @Cinderelllllaa

You taught us to be

Thank you for the opportunity to display
positivity and growth in all situations.

Marie

A send off to the year
the new one will bring us cheer
but don't wait 'till it's too late
celebrate now
we have a world to create.

Keva G
IG- @_keva_g

Thank you for teaching me to
finally like beer.

All those nights in lockdown, then all the
days in the parks and then finally outdoor
dining. What can I say I never drank more
alone, socially distant, eventually with
friends at tables because all the other
activities I love haven't been able to
reconvene. I have to say it deepened my
friendships. And the beer even started to
grow on me. Nothing like a cold Modelo
Especial! Here's a shout-out to the Bronx
Brewery, Bronx DraftHouse, and all the
mami and papi bodegas that keep the good
stuff flowing.

Laurie Jane
IG- @lauriejane.lj

If you're reading this... DRINK UP
cus a-lot of shit went down...
You lived, saw and conquered
2020 Cheers 2 You

Karyn (Celeb)
IG/Twitter- @thesilentceleb

Our parties were cancelled,
plans fell through, dates postponed and yet
we raged against the machine.
Raise your beer! Thank You 2020,
you showed us, no matter the distance,
we are still better together, Bronx Forever

How did we all make it through this year?
I don't know but I know that our
communities became stronger.
Our relationships with each other became
clearer than ever before.
This year leveled the playing ground,
but those of us that are still standing are
looking forward.

Gabriel Rosangel
IG- @ChartreuseDaddy

Dear 2020,

As we come to the end of this road I want to
thank you for the reminder that we are all
subject to change.
The world, society and myself.
You are living proof that one cannot deny
that the unforeseen is right around the
corner and the excuse 'I was unprepared' will
never hold weight again. You have taught the
lesson to embrace the truth, love and joy that
exists. You have given reason to hug tighter,
love harder, speak louder and to walk lighter.
You have shown the power of knowledge and
unity. And it allows me to look forward to
the day when I drift on the memory when
you were me and I was you. But in the
meantime and in-between time, farewell &
be swell.

Marysol
IG- @_marysol

Yeah, no sharks. No earthquakes either.
At last check, all nuclear power plants are
not on fire.
So, it could've been worse.

John Zufall

2020- Isolated yet Reconnected

Mark Brown

Don't let 12/31 hit your a$$ on the way out

Steven Waxman
IG- @il418

Can't keep us down!

This year challenged us all in endless ways.
We will come out the other side stronger
than we ever knew.

Yvonne
IG- @yapnyc

2020, You were the best of the worst.
I shared a first kiss and got down with this
guy I've been crushing on for years.
But you didn't have to do RBG like that,
or bring COVID upon the world.

The guy was my very first crush in
elementary school.
We're almost thirty now.
#RIPRBG

Anonymous Bronx Girl

137

What up 2020,
I really was feeling you for the first couple of
months but then came March and you
f*cked sh*t up. I didn't like what you were
bringing to the table, but I thought about it
and I gotta admit… you made me stronger
and I discovered a lot about myself.
So yeah, I guess we're still cool.
Just don't do this ish again.

Jennifer Pinilla
IG- @jpriscilla

A good beer reminds me the world is still a
great place so my therapist recommended
this.

Aric Yackly

in spite of the distance. the fear.
the "i don't know's if you'll be here,
tomorrow."
we here. wondrously alive.

ATABEY
IG- @atabey.rev
Twitter- @atabeyrev

Dear 2020,
The moment is never over
It always exist but can we make 2020 feel as
hazy as this

Dear 2020,
I just want to be hoppy.

Dear 2020,
Theres A lot of truth in just…
Just take it back 2020

Dear 2020,
I'm Team God

Dear 2020,
Thank you for reminding us it's all or
nothing !

Dear 2020,
Where's my beer ?

Dear 2020,
Drink Beer.

Letdowns and Let go

Dear 2020
This is how my feels flow

Hugs and long beautiful stares
How could we forget a touch is priceless
This year stands alone
Nothing compares
Love is never gone
Just different now.
The feelings that have become more
grounded are the ones not wanting this
anymore.
Life, I love you with all my heart but this isn't
what I want.
Nothing is feeding my soul
Making me happy or plain and simple I don't
want what this has become
Time will allow us to align with what we say
and do
Very important attributes
of a man I might say
But do we have time anymore?
Right now you just can't give us what we
need, you haven't even been able to give that
to yourself.
We all have taken too much

Dear 2020 and Mother Earth I'm sorry we
just take and worry about wealth
This year you reminded everyone it's about
health
It's about you
It's funny how these weird situations pull you
towards the right direction.
I been looking for love in the wrong places
because my love is all I need .
Love is all you need
Although you hurt millions
I can find absolutely nothing wrong with
you.
As I grow, the change always hurts
We'll just call it growing pains.
Just that this one really really hurts.

Miosotty Hiciano
IG- @miovelli

Whachumean?!

DISME!

OYE 2020!! ESCUCHA PORQUE SOLO TE
VOY A DECIR ESTA VES...
QUE DIABLO TU CREES QUE ES ESTE
MUNDO? SABES QUE TU AS
DESTROZADO MUCHAS VIDAS?
EL MUNDO COMPLETO ESTA EN
ESTADO DE SHOCK POR TI!
PENSE QUE ENTRABAS EN PAZ Y
LUEGO NOS DIMOS CUENTA QUE TU
VENIAS CON TU PROPRIA IDEA DE
CUENTAS. ESTOY TAN ENOJADA POR
TODO EL DAÑO CAUSADO,
HABLO POR TODOS LO QUE NO
PUEDIERON TENER EL MOMENTO DE
HABLAR CON O VER SUS FAMILIARES,
NO ME IMAGINO EL MIEDO QUE
PASARON Y TAN DE REPENTE.
AVECES ME DAN GANAS DE LLORAR
TAN FUERTE POR EL MUNDO,
POR LA PERDIDA DE MI HERMANO Y
LAS TRAJEDIAS QUE SE PRESENTARON.
NO TE ODIO, PERO SI TE QUIERO

FUERA YA BASTA ES TIEMPO QUE TE
VAYAS LEJOS DE AQUI!
VETE Y NO VUELVAS JAMAS!!! PUTO

Miguelina
IG- @msniastylez

The crazy #$%& 2020.

Chi Chen
IG- @Jchen0229
Twitter- @Iamchen_

Bye Bye 45! Hello 46!

Leanne Stella
IG- @Leanne_Stella
Twitter- @Leannestella

Everything has happened so fast & slow at
the same time.
Time— does not exist and apparently neither
do I, as I struggle to understand my purpose
& meaning in life.
But I do have to thank you.
For making me live every day like if it's my
last.

Kirstie Saunders
IG- @writer.saunders
Twitter- @_writersaunders

Pinky High to the gods.

No matter what happened this year can't stop
the BX from being legendary

King Neptune
IG- @kingneptune_nfe

Year 2020 -
Where failure met ambition & passion!!
This year is where every doubt I had as a
child became true.
Watching the Bronx in the last few months
brought back memories of the late 1900s.
When they go low , The Bronx goes high.
We let our ambition and passion to change
the world reflect further than a face
covering. We stopped at nothing to protect
our own. We came together in a time of
need.
Cheers to 2020, thanks for the character
buildup!!

J Roddy
IG- @DaBodegaUnion

Si-Ya-Rona!!!
To 2020 You WONT BE MISSED!!!!

Zelina Martinez
IG- @wwz331

2020 CAN HOLD A FRANK!
2020K RIP TO ALL MY REAL ONES
WE LOST THIS YEAR!
SHOUTOUT MY BRONX FAMILY BIG BX
VIBES! IF YOU MADE IT OUT OF 2020
YOU BETTER CHASE YA DREAMS
DEADASS - MR. BRONX ANTICS

Bronx Antics
IG- @BronxAntics

Lessons repeat until lessons are learned.
20 then 20 again,
A black hole that sucked us in
Shame on you, shame on them,
Shame on me.
Choosing to be fooled again blissfully.
Yet contrary to popular belief,
Being who we are is exactly what we're
supposed to be.
Lessons repeat until lessons are learned.
What misconceptions did 2020 burn?
The time is now, I don't have to wait my turn.
The invitation to greatness is nameless,
we're building character by working through
the vagueness.
Ushering us a step closer to our truths.
The world will never be the same, let's start
something new.
The hero we need also lives inside of you.
Who knew? Locked at home, hoping for
freedom in a voting booth.
Power to the people, we always got the juice.
Haters keep a facade like it's their job.
We don't do corny over here, save that shit
for the cob

The work begins within, to heal ourselves
and move past our sins.
If we lose all hope then this year is sure to
win.
Today does not control the fate of tomorrow.
Yesterday's displayed to reminding us we'll
blow away if we're hollow.
Swallowed our pride, put a mask on to
survive.
If we can run through this battlefield,
tomorrow we just might fly.
This is fate. Mama said, when the universe
says "yes" it's already too late.
So why is our greatness up for debate?
Things have gone wrong but we still in
Harlem with the shake.
Headed uptown just to get the boogie down
Bronx ain't burnin' but the heat all over town
Still we coolin' from Brooklyn to Staten Isle,
while the Queens wear their crown.
New York strong, built to last, pour a glass.
2020 too, shall pass.

Julissa Contreras
IG/Twitter- @jewleesah

Hop on Board!
Bronx Brewery Beer is 2020 Vision.

Daniel Lanzilotta
IG- @DanielLanzilotta

155

Dear 2020,
You stole my best friend, halted my career
and tried to take my self worth.
But what you didn't know was that,
I come from the concrete jungle,
where I learned to survive.
Your gaslighting tactics didn't break me...
they just made me thrive.
#bronxgirlinportland

Jen
IG/Twitter- @JenSoFly

Fu@$ You! You're fired!

Joe Rienti
IG- @Joey_riri

Etu Brute 2020

Yaz here, let me catch you up on what's been
going on. Came back from my first
international trip, was depressed, got better,
got Baptized with my Church, started
graduate school for my MFA in poetry,
strengthened my relationship with God,
spent time with family and friends, started a
new job, celebrated a ton of birthdays and
holidays, set fake new years resolutions,
loved my new job, started second semester of
grad school, pandemic hit, lost my job,
school went to shambles, hit financial
struggles, got isolated from friends and
family when my love language is quality
time, became a plant mom, renovated my
room, got depressed again but this time with
my self image, got better, started a KETO
lifestyle, launched a cosmetics line as part of
my business Poetic Yaz, was in a hit and run
car accident a few days before my birthday,
friends planned an amazing birthday week
I'll never forget, went to a drive in movie,
started taking photography more seriously,
got into a funk after my car accident and

needed to heal, started physical therapy, launched a BRONX dinner party along others as part of my church, started my second year of grad school, made it to a pool this summer & roasted marshmallows over a fire pit all in the same day, assimilating back into a normal routine, did a Daniel Fast and it was HARD, spending time with loved ones, starting to feel good about myself again, love my hair again, and now I'm here, it's November and I'm trying to enjoy life.

Don't know for how long but I'm soaking it in.

Yasmilka Clase
IG- @creatively.yaz
Twitter- @PoeticYaz

If you can imagine it, it is real.

Whatever you can visualize and create in
your mind and heart you can bring into
reality. It doesn't matter where you come
from. What matters is where you want to go.
Keep your spark alive!

Elias Ortiz
IG- @eliasortiz.trpt
Twitter- @eliasortiztrpt

Been there, done that.
Peace out 2020.
Thou shalt not chinstrap.
What would Cuomo Do?

Faith Sone

2020 you been a gift and a curse.

A blessing and a quiet break for reflection and realization as to what's important, to me, and I think more importantly to the collective.

Bianca Guzman
IG/Twitter- @msrapstress

2020 you came, you saw and you did not
conquer... still standing, still strong!
You hit us hard with a disease, death, hate
and intolerance.
But we still fight, we still love and we still
survive.
New York strong. Bronx strong.

Madeline Ramos
IG- @pinkladyofGod
Twitter- @Maddie_love78

Dear 2020 - I was supposed to go to Japan this year. That didn't happen. I was supposed to be my best self this year. That didn't happen either. But at the same time, it did happen. I found God and a new love and worked out more than I ever did before. But I also gained the most amount of weight this year and fell into a bad depression that I'm not sure even went away yet.

I've lived 12 lifetimes in just 12 months. I'm done with you 2020, but I'm also grateful for you. You make no sense to me 2020. You're a paradox, 2020. You make my head hurt, 2020. For real, please leave through the front door and let 2021 in, thanks.

Josue Mendez
IG- @no.way.josue
Twitter- @yeswayjosue

2020 was like finally writing that paper we
had been procrastinating on;
the paper of change, justice, equality, and
lessons learned.
The voice that we had held in for so long
only to come bursting out beautifully,
making all the difference

Ammara
IG- @Keepinthesunlightt

2020 you tested our BX Strong but Still We Rise, Yerrrrr!!!

Melissa Caraballo
IG- @Stellar__m

2020 showed up like the drunk tio causing
debauchery, no time to turn off the lights,
we're all home.
We inhaled all your blows, followed by beer
after beer.
Now no one is sober but we're woke.
Exhaling you out. Good riddance!

2020 showed up & we had no time to throw
caution towards the wind.
Between politics & losing an unfathomable
amount of beings & natural disasters,
nothing has shocked us anymore... but
thank you for unveiling layers of life, people,
things and ourselves that called for much
needed nurturing. Most importantly our
priorities & mental health.
Giving us the opportunity to get right from
within so we can be stronger together. Xoxo

Natasha Garcia
IG- @Natblack_

2020 has been rough.

Wait that's an understatement.

It's probably made us cry more tears and drip more sweat than all of our years combined. But more importantly 2020 was raw and it opened more wounds than we knew we could handle. And guess what?

We're handling it.. barely but we are alive aren't we? & one thing is for sure - it's opened our eyes to the work that still needs to be done. And we know there is quite a lot of work. But it has left us stronger so that we can fight for the world we want and know that we are capable of handling whatever else comes at us. So to that I say is that all you got, 2020?

Jasmine
IG/Twitter- @Jasmine_elissa

May we get what we want but may we never
get what we deserve.

Diego Leon
IG/Twitter- @dandyinthebronx

Dear 2020,

One too many Coronas made you a better
one night stand than a "morning after"
Brunch date for Mimosas. Still, I want to say
thank you for making me come through my
senses… more than once.

Weekend shots of Tequila, chased by the
memories of when outside was open
were warm companions and when a swipe
right couldn't contend with your quarantine.
The captivity of your presence didn't allow
for my favorites, so even on good days Rum
& Pineapple were only reminders that I
couldn't drink freely with a clear conscience.
You gave me survivor's guilt mixed with a
survivor's reluctant gratitude. Gin & Jay's
being easier on my stomach than the news
most times, but I wouldn't have it any other
way. The pauses you've afforded me brought
me an abundance of presence, nurturing my
creativity and opening my third eye to the
greatest gifts of life.

My purpose, my family, and my happiness
are three things I will never take for granted
again. No Modelo, but I'm walking away
from you as the baddest bitch I've ever been.

Cheers

theViine
IG- @theviine
Twitter- @lovealigns

Take your 'Rona!
Take your 'lection!
We are f*ckin' done!
Bring the sunshine, bring some love,
Bring on '21!

Laraine
IG- @soulpoetree

Brevity can be poignant
And crossed paths can still affect future forks
in the proverbial road
Stay firm, Feet rooted
in your purpose, your space
Let the spirit & the heart steer this
Journey in Faith

Jessica Diaz
IG- @jboogie193

How The City Survived

Some worked, and some played.
Some had to ride the train while others their
bikes.
The ones that couldn't do either hailed
yellow cabs
and they ordered their coffee the same way,
at the same time, from the same place.
Things had slowed down, but still, some of
us rushed.
All of us waited.

We waited for a sign that things would get
back to normal.
Many of us learned to long for the things we
once hated.
We missed the noisy traffic, the busy streets,
the crowded trains,
and a few even missed the slow-walking
tourists in front of the Empire State Building,
but everyone still hated "Empire State of
Mind" by Jay-Z.

We drank in public and dined in the heat, in
the rain, and later in the cold,

sometimes with friends and sometimes
alone.
Kids had birthday parties in the park, and
couples went on picnic dates,
while the rest of us told stories on fire
escapes and sang on rooftops.

Old friends, now strangers, crossed paths,
"It's been so long," a few of them said.
Grandmothers strolled into empty bodegas,
and grown men heard the echoes of their
laughter
as they walked past shuttered barbershops.
Regulars ate at their favorite restaurants,
unknowingly, for the last time.
Some escaped to where they came from
while the rest of us had no place else to go.

But when they ask us how we got through it,
we'll all respond,
"By being the greatest city in the world."

Carlos Matias
IG- @Shawtylos
Twitter- @_Loso

2020 is only good in hindsight.

Jake Alrich

"DO NOT ENTER"
-Time Travelers BEWARE

Steven Almeida
IG/Twitter- @___Therealworld

I don't know how long this'll last
so kiss me through your face mask.
Send me the morse code of your heart
so I can feel it from six feet apart.
Hold me closer in your dreams
And I'll see you after quarantine.

Bryan Orbe
IG- @Semper_bry

2020- Ding Dong the Demon is gone
2021-Life will go on.
Da Bronx stands Forever.

DèLise Temple
IG- @empressmedusa

2020 was everyone's worst fears come true, but we strived and survived and pushed through. May we all continue to grow and love through this bad moment in our journey called life.

Ruddy Mejia
IG- @See_obscure

So long,
Farewell,
Year Gone Hazy 2020,
Counted our blessings,
But lessons aplenty,
Seen some ups,
Some downs,
Always smiled,
Never see us frown,
We from Da' Bronx baby,
Our Timbs on solid ground,
NY logo fitted,
Soldier fix that crown,
Year Gone Hazy 2020,
Taught me who to let go of,
And who to keep,
Through it all,
I just tried to be the best version of me,
Socially distant,
Consistent,
Did what we had to,
Thankful to be still in existence,
Reminisce on those we lost,
Can't never forget em,
No negative energy in our circle,
Those squares we wouldn't let them,

Caught up in the journey,
Trying to stay the course,
Living the life that we were meant to,
At any cost…

Julio Jordan
IG/Twitter- @luckycesar

Don't be fooled by the divide and conquer
strategies masquerading what the truth is.
We been living with injustice,
being complacent
We all allowed it to fester in the background
due to the looming fear that this is our
reality.
Whispers of what can change, if anything.
But now it's become harder to ignore the
cracks within our society
We say their names to remind us that their
deaths are not natural
That WE are them and THEY are us
Silence has become our death
We let history dictate what our future will be
This is not our American Dream
We cannot stay dreaming of what may be.

Esther Rosa
IG- @Blkdominikana

2020 was a year of reflection,
Was the year we learned the world doesn't
revolve around our attention,
Was the year that we understood we took for
granted Gods given protection,
Was the year my father died and it taught me
a lesson.
It taught me that God is there even at your
lowest, (lois)
And we're Superman with no kryptonite
even with our demons closest
Nothing can take us down
we don't even need to focus,
Because God is working things out even
when you don't know it,
So moving forward I ain't got no time for the
disappointments
Plus I got internal demons that be "jumping"
that I'm kriss and krossing
I now gain control when things get crazy
So nobody can win even when the
years gone hazy.

Uni-G
IG/Twitter- @iAmUniG

2020 thank you for the challenges.
Without experiencing them,
I wouldn't be here today.
But we can't be friends.

Kimberly
IG- @_kmberlyr

You can't X out the X.
The Bronx is Bouncing Back.

Maurice Hurd
IG- @mosthealthybronx
Twitter- @MostHealthyBX

2020- The year we never saw coming and glad to see leaving!!

Bishop
IG- @Bishop.005

This is the year, the year we will all
remember. We collectively all experienced so
much together while not actually being with
each other. Trauma, loss, joy - we've had it all
together and apart. We had a revolution.
A revolution of black voices.
A revolution of power.
A revolution of health, of science, of truth.
I hope history will be kind to us but in this
moment hope and faith are strong.
We are strong. Alone & together, connected
& apart.

Sonia
IG- @Houseofsours

You destroyed illusions.
You removed distractions.
And you pulled the wool back from our eyes.
You forced us to focus on what matters,
and not believe the easy lies we tell ourselves.
And you proved, loudly, that we're all in this
together.

Kevin Scheitrum
IG/Twitter- @Scheity

2020 came with the lowest lows and highest highs. A long and beautiful year that made us grow and look beyond.
One for the books, let's raise a glass for the memories, it's all about the journey so let's keep going!

Amaurys Grullon
IG/Twitter- @amaurysgrullon

2020, you have been a wild roller coaster ride for me.

This year started off with the most intense beginning of a new decade I've ever seen or heard of. Geo-political tensions rising overseas in January due to a certain event occurring. A pandemic engulfing our country in the span of a few weeks. A spring and summer that will most likely be remembered for its heartaches, social issues, and communities coming together in times of strife. Finally, a fall and winter that could be described as the most polarized presidential election in American history-in my personal opinion.

However, I've learned a lot this year, which I will carry with me for a long time. I've learned that our communities and neighbors sometimes must work together when the world is falling apart around us. I've learned that we must be aware of how the systems around us work and how we can best address the issues plaguing our neighborhoods if we want to get things back in order. Finally, I've learned that even when everything seems so cynical, there is still some good in this world that still resonates in others.

Hopefully, the future gets better. Here's to 2021.

Haneiro Perez

Message from the editor

After such an extraordinary year, we're excited to create a piece of interactive art that allows our people to express themselves while enjoying a beer. Thank you to all who submitted. The phrases made me laugh, reflect, smile, and weep. Some expressed hopefulness and frustration with the ongoing fight for black lives. Some described their anger and grief with Covid-19. While others found love, purpose, and tranquility. Our goal with BX Writers is to highlight and showcase the storytellers in our community and this project furthered that initiative.

This collaboration with the Bronx Brewery & Bronx Native is a special one.

BX Writers/ Josué Caceres

Message from Bronx Native

YERRRRR! One thing that we have been able to do through Bronx Native is bridge the gap between art, culture, and our community. This project is a perfect example of that. This collaboration with The Bronx Brewery & BX Writers is a time capsule that will capture the historic year that is 2020. This is the voice of our people.

Bronx Native/ Amaurys Grullon

Message from The Bronx Brewery

We've always said that we believe in beer's ability to bring people together and 2020 redefined what that meant. Without being able to literally be together for months and months, our BXB Family found so many new and inspiring ways to stay connected. So when we thought about how to wrap up a year unlike anything we've ever experienced, we wanted to find a way to use beer to connect the voices and the people around us in a defining way. Our community is at the center of everything we do and we're so excited to work with Bronx Native & BX Writers to give people a canvas where they can send off 2020.

The Bronx Brewery/ Damian Brown

BIOGRAPHIES

BX Writers

BX Writers is a platform that highlights and showcases writers from The Bronx and its sister boroughs. BX Writers started in

February 2018 with the belief that representation is important and that the community has a story to tell. BX Writers has hosted open mics, poetry events, book clubs, workshops, and has published the BX Writers Anthology.

Bronx Native

A brand that embodies what The Bronx truly is. Highlighting The Bronx through art, media, apparel, events, and more. Changing the narrative and showcasing BX excellence.

The Bronx Brewery

The Bronx Brewery believes in beer's power to build community. We're committed to using what we create and where we create it to bring people together; while celebrating the rich and diverse creative scene in our home borough and across New York City.

Revolving around the pillars of community, creativity and inclusivity, our goal each day is to create a diverse and vibrant culture. We use beer, art, food and music to inspire, unite and drive positive change in our world.

RESOURCES

BX Writers

Instagram-@bxwriters

Facebook- BX Writers

Email- josue@bronxnative.com

Bronx Native

Instagram- @thebronxnative

Facebook- The Bronx Native

Twitter- @bxnative

Website- bronxnative.com

Email- info@bronxnative.com

The Bronx Brewery

Instagram- @thebronxbrewery

Facebook- The Bronx Brewery

Twitter- @thebronxbrewery

Website- thebronxbrewery.com

Email- info@thebronxbrewery.com